The Five Stages of Incarceration

2nd Edition

WORKBOOK &
30-DAY JOURNAL

Lester Young

ISBN: 9798417884740

Cover Design: TJ's Elements
Edited By: Youngs Solutions LLC.

This workbook is for educational purposes only and not to be taken as medical advice or a substitute for the advice and therapeutic relationship with a trusted professional.

Published by:
Youngs Solutions LLC.

TABLE OF CONTENTS

INTRODUCTION

My name is Lester Young. At the age of 19, I was sentenced to 20 years in prison. After serving 22 years and 5 months, I was granted parole. During my time of incarceration, I focused on the day I would stand before the parole board. There was a 3% chance that an individual serving a LIFE SENTENCE would be granted parole. I was determined to be within that 3%. Despite my situation, I knew I had to change my perspective.

Coming into my 3rd year of incarceration, I read books focused on understanding triggers, and the reason triggers are easy for someone, with my lifestyle prior to prison, to easily pick up with. I did not want this to later be a problem for me with parole, nor did I want to walk away from prison dealing with the same issues that I had prior to prison. The hardest step was to first acknowledge that I had underlying issues preventing my growth. I narrowed everything thing down into 5 phases/stages and began journaling.

To openly engage in conversation was something I had extreme difficulty with. Journaling was my way of having a conversation and not being judged or mocked. After successfully journaling for 30 days, I felt an instant sigh of relief and was able to move
forward, knowing that my past was no longer a hindrance for the vision of my future.

Today, I am a Transformational Life Coach. I speak to those that are currently and formerly incarcerated on how I addressed my "5 stages of incarceration". I am also the author of "The 5 Stages of Incarceration", and "The 5 Stages of Growth". I designed this workbook for those that want to reduce stress or anxiety and track their growth process while gaining a greater sense of confidence and self-identity.

Consistency is key. In order for this workbook to benefit you, it is a "MUST" that you put forth every effort in completing skill assessments, exercises, and the daily journaling.

Are you ready to address your stages of incarceration? Let us begin!

WHO QUESTIONS? PART 1

1. If you could be anyone in the world, who would you be and why?

____

____

____

2. Who could you treat better?

____

____

____

3. Who were you in the past?

____

____

____

4. Who do you put a mask on for?

____

____

____

DENIAL

When individuals are in denial, they are trying to protect themselves by refusing to accept the truth about something that is happening or about to change in their life.

Denial is the unwillingness to address or acknowledge core issues that affect your decisions, behavior, and choices. It is used as a defense mechanism to block hurt, painful memories, or accountability for one's actions. You are in denial when you experience or display any of the following:

a. Won't acknowledge a difficult situation.

b. Pretend that everything is or will be good.

c. Justify your behavior.

d. Persist in behavior despite negative consequences.

e. Suppress emotions.

f. Try not to face the facts of a problem.

g. Downplay consequences of the issue.

h. You refuse to talk about the problem.

i. Blaming others for your troubles.

j. Comparing your situation to that of others.

k. Hopeless with future planning.

l. Unwillingness to search for solutions to solve the problem.

Short-term denial can sometimes be a good thing. It can provide time to adjust to a painful or stressful situation. This type of denial is a helpful response to how you assess stressful information. If denial persists, it prevents you from taking appropriate action that could initially cause the problem to get worse than what it initially started out to be.

3 TYPES OF DENIAL

1. *Simple* denial is denying that something unpleasant is or may happen.

   Example: an individual has just received a medical diagnosis that could mean death.

2. *Minimization* is admitting knowledge of an occurrence/event but denying the seriousness.

   Example: Receiving a final warning about your job performance and denying termination may follow if no improvement.

3. *Projection* is knowing the seriousness but blaming someone else for the outcome.

   Example: Understanding the final warning from your job is based on you keeping your job given you improve your performance, but you blame the manager for not making changes to the way the job is done.

CAUSES OF DENIAL

1. *Abandonment* -Deserting the caregiving needs of an individual while neglecting to arrange sufficient care and support for the duration of the absence.
2. *Abuse* -Misuse to bad effect or for a bad purpose
3. *Addiction* -Craving for something intensely, loss of control over its use, and continuing involvement with it despite adverse consequences.
4. *Anxiety* -A feeling of fear, dread, and uneasiness
5. *Grief* -A deep sorrow, trouble, or annoyance
6. *Fear* -An idea of intense reluctance to face or meet a person or situation
7. *Insecurity* -Lack of Confidence

Denial might be a coping mechanism that prevents an individual from facing a problem. If you are dealing with denial, the first thing you should do is think about the reasons you are afraid to face the problem. Honestly identify and examine what it is you fear. identify the thoughts that might be contributing to your fear. Allow yourself to express your fears and emotions by addressing all irrational beliefs. Then consider the consequences involved if you choose not to deal with the problem.

Sometimes talking with someone you trust, and respect can provide some relief. Listening to their advice can provide a different prospective and/or view. If expressing your emotions is not your strong area, than write down what you are experiencing on paper or in a journal.

EXERCISE #1

In the scenarios below, identify the type of denial is being displayed:

1. "I'm having an affair, so what" ____________________

2. "I'm not taking this medication; I don't care if it does control my blood pressure"

   ____

3. "I have cancer, which doesn't mean I'm going to die"

   ____

4. "The affair would not have happened if you didn't take a trip with your friends" ____________________

5. "You're mad at me because I got into a car accident, if you would have taken me to the store then this would not have happened"

   ____

6. "I drink alcohol every day that doesn't affect my work performance, so what's the big deal"

   ____

EXERCISE #2

Below are 12 **"Patterns of Denial".** Match each term with the correct definition on the following page.

1. Avoidance ______
2. Absolute Denial ______
3. Blaming ______
4. Comparing ______
5. Compliance ______
6. Democratic Disease State ______
7. Flight Into Health ______
8. Manipulating ______
9. Minimizing ______
10. Rationalizing ______
11. Recovery by Fear ______
12. Strategic Hopelessness ______

a. "I have the right to destroy myself and no one can stop me"
b. "Being scared of my problems makes them go away"
c. "I will only admit to having problems if you agree to solve them for me"
d. "He/She does way more wrong then I do, what I've done is nothing"
e. "If I can prove that my problems are not my fault, I won't have to deal with them"
f. "Who me?" I do not have any problems
g. "I'll talk about whatever you want except my own problems"
h. "My problems are not that bad"
i. "If I can find good enough reasons for my problems, I won't have to deal with them"
j. "I'll pretend to do what you want, if you leave me alone"
k. "I feel a lot better so that means there's nothing wrong"
l. "I've tried everything, and nothing works"

ABOUT YOU

1. Are you currently suffering from denial?

   ____

2. What is the reason(s) you suffer from denial?

   ____

   ____

3. Out of the 7 causes of denial, which one relates directly to you and why?

   ____

   ____

   ____

   ____

4. Do you have someone with whom you can talk?

   ____

5. How often do you talk with this person?

   ____

6. What advice would you share with someone displaying the signs of denial?

   ____

   ____

7. What are some take away points from this chapter that will help you on your journey?

   ____

   ____

WHO QUESTIONS? PART 2

1. Who do you aspire to be? Why?

2. Who influenced you as a child?

3. Who has caused you the most pain?

4. Who do you surround yourself with? Why?

ANGER

A normal human reaction, anger can be effective in certain situations. While responding to threats of injury or harm to yourself or others, but NOT being able to control anger, can quickly turn destructive and cause problems in your life, as well as negatively affect personal and professional relationships.

Before being consumed with anger, an individual experiences a primary emotion, such as fear, loss, or sadness. Primary emotions allow us to feel vulnerable, uncomfortable, and allow us to lose control. Anger is a secondary emotion. It is a mixture of fear, shame, and sometimes fueled with issues of betrayal, abandonment, abuse, and rejection.

FORMS OF ANGER

1. *Direct* -Anger towards the one that inflicted pain or injury.
2. *Indirect* -Causing pain to others because of the pain someone has caused you.
3. *Unresolved* -Resentment, bitterness towards the person that caused you pain.
4. *Inward* - Directed internally, dark depressing thoughts and negative self-talk
5. *Outward* -Expressing anger verbally or physically toward other people and things.
6. *Passive* -Passive-aggressive behavior, sarcastic or degrading toward others, giving others the silent treatment, and sulking.

Individuals that are constantly angry will display some or all the following personality traits:

a. A fragile ego (sense of self-esteem or self-importance)
b. Entitlement (believing that one's rights and privileges are superior to those of other people)
c. Focusing on things out of your control
d. Trying to regulate emotions by controlling one's environment

e. Believing well-being is controlled by sources outside of oneself
f. Viewing different perspectives as threats

Anger is exposed when someone or something triggers a response or emotion. A trigger is anyone, or anything that can instantly cause tension. Some common triggers are:

- Being blamed for something you did not do
- Being insulted
- Disrespect to you or your property.
- Injustice in an argument or dispute.
- Violation of personal space.
- Physical threats.
- Misinformation.

4 STAGES OF ANGER

1. *The Buildup* -the foundation in which anger is built (stems from)
2. *The Spark* -gesture or phrase that ignites tension or violent behavior
3. *The Explosion* -express strong feelings suddenly and violently.
4. *The Aftermath* -negative consequences resulting from verbal or physical aggression displayed

Controlling anger can be extremely difficult. When you are in the moment, you usually do not have time to think clearly or rationally, but you can control how you express your anger. The first step is recognizing your warning signs. Start paying attention to how you are feeling. If caught early, you can take the proper steps of preventing your anger from reaching a boiling point. Another outlet is talking with a friend, loved one, or someone who can instantly calm you down while you are in the moment. Discussing your feelings MAYBE helpful, but it is safe to note that sometimes "venting" can backfire. In circumstances such as this, it may be best to keep a journal. That way, the stress and frustrations are released from you without sharing the experience with someone that could add more fumes to an already burning flame.

TIPS TO MANAGE ANGER

1. Breathe in deeply, filling up your abdomen, wait a few seconds then breathe out. Repeat this step 3 times if needed.
2. Exercise/Stretch
3. Counting backwards is a great technique. The number you start from should be based on the level of anger you are expressing. The higher the number, the calmer you will become.
4. Despite what is going on, try envisioning yourself in your happiest moment, or happiest place.
5. Remove yourself by taking a time out.
6. Think of other solutions that could easily deescalate the situation from becoming worse.
7. Think about the consequences in the event you act upon your anger.
8. Do not hold a grudge.
9. Use humor to release tension.
10. Listen to calming music
11. Repeat a peaceful saying
12. Practice gratitude
13. Journal your feelings
14. Practice empathy
15. Paint or draw

EXERCISE #1

Fill in the blanks

1. What stage of anger is expressed as a "gesture" or phrase the ignites tension or violent behavior?
   a. The Explosion
   b. The Buildup
   c. The Spark
   d. The Aftermath

2. Which one of the following IS NOT a tip in dealing with anger?
   a. Use humor to release tension
   b. Counting backwards
   c. Remove yourself
   d. Engage in profanity and escalate the situation

3. What is a trigger?
   a. Anyone or anything causing tension
   b. Someone disrespecting you
   c. Being told information to insight confusion
   d. All the above

4. What are 2 forms of anger?
   a. Direct & Indirect
   b. Formal & Nonformal
   c. Resolved & Sideward
   d. Temperamental & Persuasive

5. Anger is a _______ emotion.
   a. Primary
   b. Secondary
   c. Temporary
   d. Calming

6. Anger is displayed in which personality trait?
   a. Entitlement
   b. Journaling
   c. Having Empathy
   d. Talking to a friend

7. If you have difficulty talking to someone or suspect the talk could cause more harm than help, what should you try
   a. Hold your feelings inside
   b. Take out your frustrations on others
   c. Shut down
   d. Log your feelings/thoughts in a journal

EXERCISE #2

Being prepared before dealing with anger is a great way to plan for any situation. Fill in the boxes below to "Prep for Anger."

1. What is the situation?

____

____

____

____

2. What makes me angry?

____

____

____

____

3. What are some things I can do to prepare for this situation?

____

____

____

____

____

4. How I would I have managed this in the past?

____

____

____

____

____

5. What are the signs that I am getting angry?

____

____

____

6. Coping Skills, I can use if I start to feel angry.

____

____

____

ABOUT YOU

1. Do you feel you have issues with anger? If so, which form of anger describes you?

   ____

   ____

   ____

2. How do you control your anger?

   ____

   ____

   ____

3. What personality trait (common in anger) relates to you the most and why?

   ____

   ____

   ____

4. Describe a time when your anger was out of control and describe the strategies you or someone else was able to calm the situation down.

   ____

   ____

   ____

5. How do you respond to anger? Choose the from the list below then describe your choice(s):
    a. Yelling & Screaming
    b. Name-Calling
    c. Sad & Crying
    d. Hitting or Kicking
    e. Threatening
    f. Using Profanity
    g. Throwing Things
    h. Running Away
    i. Slamming Doors

____

____

____

____

____

____

____

____

____

____

____

____

____

____

WHO QUESTIONS? PART 3

1. Who have you witnessed being or playing a victim?

2. Who has betrayed your trust?

3. Who are the people in your circle that seek attention?

4. Who are the positive influences in your circle?

SELF-VICTIMIZATION

There are people that play victim for the choices they make, the crimes they commit, or the problems they cause that feel as if they are at the mercy of everyone around them. This issue is not only a problem of not trusting others, but a problem of the victim not believing they are trustworthy themselves. Commonly referred to as "attention seekers" that will use any excuse to NOT accept responsibility of his/her own life, choices, or circumstances.

Self-victimization is the act of blaming others for their problems. This dysfunctional mindset seeks to convince others that life is not fair and deliberately out to hurt or punish them. Their beliefs constantly result in finger-pointing, and pity parties that are fueled by pessimism, fear, and anger. If the response their looking for is not given, they can become manipulative, and vindictive, an attention seeker, and uses any excuse to NOT accept responsibility of his/her own life, choices, or circumstances.

Some common signs of identifying self-victimization mentality are:

a. You blame others for the way your life is.
b. You genuinely think life is against you.
c. You have trouble coping with problems in your life and feel powerless against them.
d. You feel stuck in life and approach things with a negative attitude.
e. Lack self-confidence.
f. Suffer with low self-esteem.
g. Things could be going wonderful, and you will still find something to complain about.
h. You refuse to find solutions to your problems.
i. You assume you are under attack when someone gives constructive criticism.
j. You search for people to befriend or be in relationships with that display the same behavior.

There are many causes to trigger this mindset. A result of ongoing emotional pain, being betrayed by someone you love or trust, various situations in which you lost control, or being victimized during their childhood. Unhealthy relationships with parents, siblings or witnessing behaviors displayed by family members, can sometimes begin the cycle leading to this toxic behavior. If the individual endured any type of abuse (emotional, physical, or sexual), then being and continuing to play victim may have been used as a coping mechanism. There are many rewards to being a victim:

1. Not having to take responsibility
2. Being lavished with attention
3. People feeling sorry for you
4. You have the "right" to complain
5. You are more likely to get what you want

The views and/or opinions of others (peers, society, social media), can encourage this behavior. When criticized about:

- Your Race
- Living in a low-income environment (poverty)
- Being raised in a 1-parent household
- Lack of education
- Characterized as a minority
    - Being denied opportunities and not being told the reasoning why

An individual may feel worthless or ashamed and use the above reasons to become a victim of their lifestyle, habits, or environment.

As much as you would like to forget whatever pain, hurt, or trauma you MAY HAVE experienced in your childhood that has caused you to self-victimize yourself, as you become an adult, you have 2 choices:

- Repeat the cycle
- Break the cycle

To move forward, you must stop blaming others for the consequences of your actions. Accept responsibility for your choices and resist sabotaging anything that is going good in your life. Practice exercises designed to build your self-confidence by replacing low self-esteem with compassion, gratitude, and self-worth. Despite your environment, continue to educate yourself to better your situation and/or circumstances so that when others plant seeds of doubt or negativity, it does not do ***ANYTHING OTHER*** than motivate you into becoming a better you.

EXERCISE #1

1. List 3 signs of self-victimization.

   a. ______________________________
      ____

   b. ______________________________
      ____

   c. ______________________________
      ____

2. List 3 causes of self-victimization.

   a. ______________________________
      ____

   b. ______________________________
      ____

   c. ______________________________
      ____

3. List 3 benefits of self-victimization.

   a. ______________________________
      ____

b. ____

____

c. ____

____

4. List 3 steps to prevent self-victimization.

a. ____

____

b. ____

____

c. ____

____

EXERCISE #2

Write the act of self-victimization each scenario describes:

1. Seeking attention from others because you live in an apartment complex is an example of ____________________.

2. Your parents are divorced so you tell your peers lies about things you do at home to avoid being neglected or left out of social events is an example of ____________________.

3. You dropped out of high school because studying was not considered the cool thing to do, while taking a test for employment, you struggle with answering some basic math questions, this is an example of ____________________.

ABOUT YOU

1. Do you or someone you know of suffer from self-victimization? If so, what do you think is the cause?

____

____

____

2. How are you with accepting responsibility for actions and facing consequences as the result of your actions?

____

____

____

3. What advice would you share with someone that displayed the symptoms of claiming to be a victim of an action they caused?

____

____

WHO QUESTIONS? PART 4

1. Who has been the easiest person to forgive?

___

___

___

2. Who is the most difficult person to forgive?

___

___

___

3. Who encourages forgiveness in your family?

___

___

___

4. Who are you holding a grudge against? Why?

___

___

___

5. Who forgives you no matter what you do?

___

___

___

FORGIVENESS

One of the hardest things to do is to show empathy or mercy towards someone that has hurt you or someone you love. It is a decision that you must live with for the rest of your life. So, you can either hold on to anger, resentment, and remain bitter or embrace forgiveness so that YOU can move forward, regardless of whether they deserve it or not!

Forgiveness empowers you to move past any hurt, pain, or guilt. It does not mean you are excusing the actions, or forgetting what circumstances took place, it means you are taking control of your life and NO longer allowing what once caused you pain to continue being a hindrance in your life.

Holding grudges, pinned up anger, and thoughts of seeking revenge can cause stress, which leads to high blood pressure, and other health problems like anxiety, or feelings of depression. When you forgive, your body releases the pressures of stress, your mood is elevated, and your perspective on how you once viewed yourself or someone changes for the better.

The act of forgiveness can show up in our lives in many stages. The most common are:

- Seeking forgiveness from God
- Seeking forgiveness from people whom you have hurt
- Seeking forgiveness from people who have hurt you
- Seeking forgiveness for yourself

1. Although asking forgiveness from God is easy, we still tend to shy away from repenting due to the pain, hurt, or grief we have caused. However, it is as simple as admitting the wrong, then simply asking forgiveness. You instantly feel relief and reassurance in knowing that God has forgiven you!

2. When seeking forgiveness from others, the first step is to offer an authentic and sincere apology. Explain the occurrence, by showing remorse and asking how you can help make the situation better.

3. Giving forgiveness to those that have hurt you can be challenging process. Try to see things from their perspective. You may have managed the situation the same. During your journey, understand you have done things and have been forgiven. Journaling can be helpful as well.

4. We can be our biggest enemy and hardest critic when it comes to forgiving ourselves. Once you have accepted responsibly of the action, allow yourself to feel guilt and/or show remorse, make amends by apologizing, learn from the situation, then begin the growth process.

Forgiveness is good for:

- ✓ Marriages
- ✓ Improving Relationships
- ✓ Resolving Conflict
- ✓ You

EXERCISE# 1

Fill in the blanks

1. ____________ leads to stress, health issues, and sometimes anxiety.
   a. Pinned Up Anger
   b. Resentment
   c. Holding Grudges
   d. All the above

2. What is the 1st step in asking forgiveness from those that we have hurt?
   a. Ask how we can make the situation better
   b. Offer an apology
   c. Explain the situation with empathy
   d. Show remorse

3. Seeking forgiveness _________ is the easiest forgiveness to ask for.
   a. From others
   b. From yourself
   c. From God

4. For whom is forgiveness ultimately?
    a. Your spouse
    b. Yourself
    c. Your friends
    d. All the above

ABOUT YOU

1. Why do you think forgiveness is more for yourself verses others?

    ____

    ____

2. Have you ever had to forgive someone that has caused you or someone you love to hurt?

    ____

    ____

3. Have you ever had to ask forgiveness from someone that YOU have hurt?

    ____

    ____

4. Is there anyone that you require forgiveness from or requires forgiveness from you?

    ____

    ____

WHO QUESTIONS? PART 5

1. Who inspires your growth? Why?

   ____

   ____

   ____

2. Who motivates you to continue being a better you? Why?

   ____

   ____

   ____

3. Who is the positive person in your circle?

   ____

   ____

   ____

4. Who is your role model? Why?

   ____

   ____

   ____

5. Who is the person you are today?

   ____

   ____

   ____

TRANSFORMATION

The process of change requires commitment. One must destroy their current habits, while mapping out an entirely new blueprint for their life. This is not an easy task, but the journey to a better you is well worth it.

Transformation is a process of change that requires lots of time and effort. While in this phase, many people become discouraged and give up on their behavior change goals. The keys to maintaining successful transformation consists of being open and practicing new techniques. To begin, you must ask yourself the following questions:

1. Have you prepared yourself with the correct tools to make this change permanent?
2. What barriers/obstacles could prevent this change from taking place?
3. What triggers may cause you to relapse?

When things you once did no longer work, no matter how hard you try, you experience feelings of confusion, reanalyze relationships/friendships, then realize you are replacing old patterns with new ones, you are entering into the stage of transformation.

Sacrifices are a "most." You will be "uncomfortable," this is needed to first recognize a change is required. Take baby steps and do not overwhelm yourself with unrealistic goals. Surrounding yourself with positivity, learning from others, and remembering to reward yourself will reassure you that you are on the right path. As with anything, total transformation is achieved once completion of the following stages have been mastered:

1. *Precontemplation* -no intention to change behavior
2. *Contemplation* -being aware that a problem exists
3. *Preparation* -information gathering, planning, most important stage.
4. *Action* -modify behavior and environment to overcome problems.
5. *Maintenance* -work to prevent relapse, and consolidate accomplishments
6. *Relapse* - a form of regression, failure to maintain because of inaction
7. *Termination* - unhealthy habit(s) no longer a way of coping.

EXERCISE #1

Fill in the blanks

1. Transformation requires ______.
   a. A partner
   b. Support system
   c. Commitment
   d. Action
2. The keys to a successful transformation are ____.
   a. Being open and practicing new techniques
   b. Recognizing the need to change and doing nothing
   c. Changing your decision and socializing with the same friends
   d. Being in denial and playing victim
3. How can you prepare yourself for transformation?
   a. Having right tools to begin.

   b. Knowing what barriers could prevent the process?
   c. What triggers could cause setback?
   d. All the above
4. When you have no intention to change your behavior?
   a. Relapse
   b. Maintenance
   c. Precontemplation
   d. Termination
5. When you work to prevent relapse?
   a. Relapse
   b. Maintenance
   c. Precontemplation
   d. Termination
6. What is the most important stage?
   a. Termination
   b. Preparation
   c. Action
   d. Relapse

EXERCISE #2

1. List 2 signs that you have started the process of transformation:
   a. ____
      ____
   b. ____
      ____
2. List the 2 signs to reassure you are on the right path:

a. ____________________

____

b. ____________________

____

ABOUT YOU

1. How have you transformed in your life?

____

____

____

____

2. How does your transformation affect your family?

____

____

____

____

3. How does your transformation affect your friends?

____

____

____

____

4. What changes did you experience in your transformation?

____

____

____

____

5. What phase of transformation are you end now?

____

____

____

____

6. What changes have you or are willing to implement to ensure your transformation is permanent?

____

____

____

____

OVERVIEW

1. Of the 5 stages, which do you associate with the most? Why?

____

____

____

2. How are you coping with this stage?

____

____

____

3. Of the 5 stages, which do you associate with the least?

____

____

____

4. What are your stages of incarceration?

____

____

____

5. How are you coping with your stages?

____

____

30-DAY JOURNAL

Not having an outlet to relieve stress can sometimes lead to mental health problems, such as depression, anxiety, and/or personality disorders. In situations like this, keeping a journal can help gain control of your emotions and improve your mental health.

Journaling is writing down your thoughts and feelings to understand them more clearly. It allows you to explore your past and envision your future. Daily journaling also helps to conquer overthinking.

For the next 30 (depending on how many days are in the month) choose a topic from the list below, write down your topic in the space provided along with the date, then begin logging your thoughts.

Journal Topics

1. What is the vision for your future and what are your plans for staying on track?
2. What areas do you want to improve and what is your timeline for seeing results?
3. How do you want to be remembered after death?
4. If you could change 1 bad experience, what would it be and how would you do it differently?
5. What are 3 goals you want to achieve and explain the process of achieving them?
6. Who is your role model and how has this person inspired your life?
7. What do you think is your purpose and what are you doing to walk in it?
8. What areas in your life are preventing your growth and how can you improve them?

9. What is your ideal career path and what makes this the right career for you?
10. What is the proudest moment in your life and who did you experience this with?
11. Write a letter to yourself when you were age 21, what advice would you give?
12. Write a letter to yourself, 10 years from now, what advice would you give?
13. How strong is your faith and are you actively practicing it?
14. Describe your relationship with your father, what would you change if you could?
15. Describe your relationship with your mother, what would you change if you could?
16. If you could meet anyone in history, who would it be, and what questions would you ask?
17. Who are 5 people in your support system, and who motivates you more?
18. If you had 24 hours to talk to a family member, alive or deceased, to ask ANY QUESTIONS you wanted, who would it be and what questions would you ask?
19. Are you holding on to grudges, if so, why and with who?
20. Do you have siblings? If so, who are you closest with and why? Who would you like to improve your relationship with?
21. Out of every lesson you have learned, which one stands out more now and who shared this lesson with you?

22. Who is the one friend you trust with anything, how long have you been friends, and how did this person earn your trust?
23. What was your greatest fear, and how did you conquer it?
24. Name something you are good at and how long have you been doing it?
25. If you could write a letter to someone that you always wanted to thank but have never had the chance to do so, who would it be and for what would you thank them?
26. What keeps you up at night worrying? Are your worries realistic? Is there anything you can do about them?
27. What is your philosophy of life or what is your method for making important decisions?
28. What is something someone else has that you envy? Describe it and your feelings about it.
29. What is a common misconception people have about you and why do you think they feel this way?
30. What is a book, movie, song, or television program that has influenced your change, and how?
31. If you could change anything about you, what would it be and how would you change it?
32. If you won the lottery, what would you do with the winnings?
33. Describe the perfect spouse, and what would you do to make sure this person is always happy and taken care of?
34. If you possessed a special power, what would it be and how would you use it?

35. What is your favorite time of the year and what memories do you have from your childhood that make that time of year so special?
36. What are your most prized possessions and why do they mean so much to you?
37. Is there something someone else has that you envy? Describe what it is and your feelings about it.
38. Where is one place that you would like to visit, and list some things you would do once you get there?

*** If there a topic you want to journal about that is not listed, feel free to do so***

Happy Journaling!!!

Journal Day 1

Date ____________________

Topic ____

Journal Day 2

Date ____________________

Topic ____

Journal Day 3

Date ____________________

Topic ____

Journal Day 4

Date ____________________

Topic ____

Journal Day 5

Date ____________________

Topic ____

Journal Day 6

Date ____________________

Topic ____

Journal Day 7

Date ____________________

Topic ____

Journal Day 8

Date ____________________

Topic ____

Journal Day 9

Date ____________________

Topic ____

Journal Day 10

Date ____________________

Topic ____________________

Journal Day 11

Date ____________________

Topic ____________________

Journal Day 12

Date ____________________

Topic ____

Journal Day 13

Date ____________________

Topic ____

Journal Day 14

Date ____________________

Topic ____

____

____

____

____

____

____

____

____

____

____

____

____

____

____

____

Journal Day 15

Date ____________________

Topic ____

Journal Day 16

Date ____________________

Topic ____

Journal Day 17

Date ____________

Topic ______________________________

Journal Day 18

Date ____________________

Topic ____

Journal Day 19

Date ____________________

Topic ____

Journal Day 20

Date ____________________

Topic ____

Journal Day 21

Date ____________________

Topic ____

Journal Day 22

Date ____________________

Topic ____

____

____

____

____

____

____

____

____

____

____

____

____

____

____

____

Journal Day 23

Date ____________________

Topic ____

Journal Day 24

Date ____________________

Topic ____

Journal Day 25

Date ____________________

Topic ____

Journal Day 26

Date ____________________

Topic ____

Journal Day 27

Date ____________________

Topic ____

Journal Day 28

Date ____________________

Topic ____

Journal Day 29

Date ____________________

Topic ____

____

____

____

____

____

____

____

____

____

____

____

____

____

____

____

Journal Day 30

Date ____________________

Topic ____

Journal Day 31

Date ____________________

Topic ____

____

____

____

____

____

____

____

____

____

____

____

____

____

____

____

ANSWER SHEET

Denial (pages 6-7)

Simple	1. G
Minimization	2. F
Simple	3. E
Projection	4. D
Projection	5. J
Minimization	6. A
	7. K
	8. C
	9. H
	10. I
	11. B
	12. L

Anger (pages 12-13)

1. C
2. D
3. D
4. A
5. B
6. A
7. D

Self-Victimization (pages 20-21)

Exercise #1

3 Signs of self-victimization

a. Blame others for the way your life is.
b. Think life is against you.
c. Have trouble coping with problems in your life and feel powerless against them.
d. Feel stuck in life and approach things with a negative attitude.
e. Lack self-confidence.
f. Low self-esteem.
g. Always complaining.
h. Refuse to find solutions to your problems.

i. Assume you are under attack when given constructive criticism.
j. Have friendships/relationships with people that display the same behavior.

3 Causes of self-victimization

- Result of ongoing emotional pain.
- Being betrayed by someone you love or trust.
- Various situations in which you have lost control.
- Being victimized during childhood.
- Unhealthy relationships with parents/siblings
- Witnessing behaviors displayed by family members

3 Benefits of self-victimization

- Not having to take responsibility
- Being lavished with attention
- People feeling sorry for you
- You have the "right" to complain
- You are more likely to get what you want

Self-Victimization (page 21)

Exercise #2

1. Victimized because of you live in a low-income environment.
2. Victimized for being raised in a 1-parent household
3. Victimized for lack of education

Forgiveness (pages 25-26)

1. D
2. B
3. C
4. B

Transformation (pages 29-30)

Exercise#1

1. C
2. A
3. D

4. C
5. B
6. B

Exercise #2 (pages 30-31)

Signs Transformation has started

When things you once did no longer work, no matter how hard you try

- Experience feelings of confusion
- Reanalyze relationships/friendships
- Replacing old patterns with new ones

Signs you are on the right path

- Take baby steps
- Do not overwhelm yourself with unrealistic goals
- Surrounding yourself with positivity
- Learning from others
- Reward yourself for every accomplishment

Made in the USA
Middletown, DE
25 October 2023